Footsteps of My Father

Everything I Know About Management I Learned From My Dad

by
Anthony Rino

authorHOUSE™

1663 LIBERTY DRIVE, SUITE 200
BLOOMINGTON, INDIANA 47403
(800) 839-8640
WWW.AUTHORHOUSE.COM

© 2005 Anthony Rino. All Rights Reserved.

No part of this book may be reproduced, stored in a retrieval system, or transmitted by any means without the written permission of the author.

First published by AuthorHouse 07/06/05

ISBN: 1-4208-6401-7 (sc)

Library of Congress Control Number: 2005905429

Printed in the United States of America
Bloomington, Indiana

This book is printed on acid-free paper.

Quote in chapter 1 taken from *They Found the Secret* by Mrs. Victor Raymond Edman. Copyright 1960 by Zondervan Publishing House. Used by permission of The Zondervan Corporation.

Dedication

To my father, who taught me
the most important values of my life:
integrity, honesty, loyalty and respect.

To my wife, Joanne,
and my children, Isabella and Nicholas,
who continually help me dream the big dreams.
I thank God every day for you.

Acknowledgments

First and foremost, I thank God
for giving me the grace to appreciate life
and the motivation to write this book.
Without You, I am nothing.

I also want to thank…

Joanne, for your unconditional love and support and your endless
source of positive energy.
You truly inspire me.
They say behind every great man is a great woman. In our case that's
not true.
You have never been behind me,
but always by my side.

My children, Isabella and Nicholas.
I loved you before you were born.
Thank you for your love and patience
while I was writing this book.
It is my gift to you.

My parents, Ralph and Josephine Rino.
You were my first teachers
about the things that matter most in life.
I am forever indebted to you both.

Ma and Dad Boudreau.
You have always welcomed me as your "son."
I will be forever grateful
for your love and support.
Thank you for who you are and all that you do.

My sisters, Nina and Anna.
Thank you for always being there
to listen and support me when I need you.
I love you both.

My other set of "sisters,"
Patti, Karen and Roseanne.
Your laughter over the years
has truly blessed my life.
Thank you for the relationships we share.

Bob, Rich, Ronnie, Mike and Antonio.
I never had a brother,
but without a doubt, you have filled that void.

Uncle Roy. Thank you for always believing in me and encouraging me
with your continued optimism.
With you, the glass is always half-full.

All my nieces and nephews.
Thank you for always reminding me
why family is so important.

Lynn and Tom Wehner.
Thank you for sharing your talents
by helping me edit this book.
I also thank you for sharing
your family, friendship and faith.
I thank God for placing us on the same road
of this incredible journey.

My mentors Ralph Rino, Mike Blanchard,
Doreen Thomas, Ed Kelly, Frank Saba,
Alice Shakman, Michele Streeter,
and John O'Brien.
Your leadership, insight, knowledge
and example are invaluable.
Thank you for showing me the way.

All my friends and family
not mentioned by name.
My life is filled with richness because of you.
You are always in my heart.

Table of Contents

Introduction		xi
Chapter 1	Find a Mentor	1
Chapter 2	Develop a Network	7
Chapter 3	Feed Your Employees	15
Chapter 4	Surpass Expectations	22
Chapter 5	Leave It at the Office	29
Chapter 6	Get in the Trenches	35
Chapter 7	Choose Wisely – You Get What You Pay For	41
Chapter 8	Do What You Love	45
Chapter 9	Don't Let Your Job Become What You Are	51
Final Thoughts		56

Introduction

Throughout my career as a manager, I have often found myself consulting the "experts" of our time on how to be a better leader. It seems that every major management textbook embraces wisdom from the Big Three – W. Edwards Deming, Joseph M. Juran and Philip B. Crosby – and I have studied nearly every concept these authors have outlined in order to improve my skills and get ahead. Let's face it, everyone knows that the fastest way to the top is to stand on the shoulders of giants that have gone before you. The thing is, although these "experts" have forever inspired me with new ways of looking at things, I have always felt in my gut that there was something missing in their brilliant lessons.

Then one day it dawned on me. It wasn't that their lessons were incomplete, but that *I* was incomplete. I was detached from my organization, professionally managing at arm's length. I was missing the battle scars that can only be earned through hands-on management. Missing the calluses born of rolling up the sleeves and getting one's hands dirty. Quite simply, I wasn't field-tested. I needed to jump off my perch and get a view of the organization from the ground up. I needed to get into the day-to-day grind once in a while and see the successes and failures first-hand.

So the next time I went looking for a role model, a so-called "expert," I decided to pick someone who led by example, not by a management formula. Someone who lived life in the trenches, not in a textbook. Fortunately for me, being the only son of an Italian immigrant, I didn't have to look far for a role model with not only a tremendous work ethic, but with a heart energized by the responsibilities of the daily journey.

Chapter 1

Find a Mentor

Footprints

It was February 1983. The ground was covered with fresh snow from the storm the night before. Though several inches of snow had fallen, there was, unfortunately for me, not enough accumulation to cancel school. I kicked myself into gear, realizing that, if I were going to make it to school on time, I would really have to rush to catch the bus.

There is something totally magical about the early morning hours after a snowstorm. The blanket of snow has a special way of quieting the world around you. In those moments, the pure silence of nature leaves you with only the sounds of your own thoughts in your head.

But as I ventured out, I had the sense that something was very different about that morning. As a freshman in high school, I had been following the same daily routine for about six months. I would get up early, eat breakfast, shower, dress and then walk up two streets to wait for my bus. I couldn't quite put my finger on what made that particular morning different, but I knew it wasn't just the gift of the snowfall. Then it hit me. I realized I was not alone on this snow-covered journey. I was sharing the path with someone who had been there before me. I knew it by the footprints left behind, preserved in the snow. The footprints started right at my own front door, and I knew, ironically, that they would lead to the same bus stop toward which I was heading. For I knew those footprints. They belonged to my dad.

For as long as I could remember, my dad would get up in the early dawn hours and make his way to the bus stop to head downtown and open up his Italian restaurant. That was my dad. He would head off to work before anyone was awake and usually return back home after most of us had gone to sleep. He was incredibly dedicated to his work, and had a firm understanding of the nature of service – offering so much of his time and energy purely for the benefit of his customers, his wife and his three children.

I remember taking deliberate steps that morning, making sure that, with each stride, my foot came down in the corresponding footprint he had left behind. After I had traveled about a block, I turned around to see the path. To anyone else venturing out that day, it would appear that only a single person had passed that way. And right then, I had a revelation. I was following in my father's footsteps – first quite literally. Each step I took traced the path pioneered by him earlier that day. But it struck me in that very moment that in my life I would have the opportunity to follow in his footsteps in other ways, as well. Most importantly, if I chose to do so and I paid close attention, I could someday follow his rigorous work ethic in my own professional life and become a loyal provider for my family.

I have no doubt that, in order to be successful in both business and life, we need to be attentive to and follow the path forged by successful individuals before us. Sure, we all need to carve out our own way through life, but learning from the lessons left behind by people we respect and love is a powerful way to start the journey. And an effective way to keep us centered as we encounter the inevitable obstacles. As for what it is to be a "success," always remember that success is wholly subjective. So find what you value most and emulate it. I have always valued so much what my dad did for our family, and have held much of his example ever before me as a path of footsteps to follow to lead me toward my definition of personal success.

Follow the Leader

Recently, I took a trip to the beach with my family. It was late in the afternoon and not particularly sunny, so the area was deserted and quiet – ideal for a peaceful stroll down the long stretch of sand. After I had walked a few hundred feet, I turned around to see my four-year-old son enthusiastically trying to follow in my sandy footprints. Obviously at a disadvantage with his small stature, he was not very accurate in his task. His stride was much shorter than mine, so he would take many extra running steps in order to make the leap to my next footprint. Looking back on the tracks of his journey, I saw anything but a perfect path, but this "follow-the-leader" game served its purpose. You see, if my son had gone too far to the left he would have been in danger from the incoming tide. And if he had gone too far to the right, he would have found himself walking on the rocks, and his journey would have been, to say the least, very uncomfortable. But as long as he stayed within my footprints, he was safe. He may not have followed my path with great accuracy, but he used it as a guide, and it kept him on course.

This experience paints the picture of what a mentor's role is all about. A mentor is one who leads by example, shows you the way, and keeps you on course. A mentor has the capability to help make the journey less dangerous and perhaps a little more comfortable. He or she doesn't do the job for you, but presents you with a model that can guide your efforts. Yes, even while following your mentor, you may stumble. But just like a child, in time your stride will widen, as you grow in confidence and experience. Combine your personal growth with a mind and heart that are focused on the right footsteps to follow, and personal success is sure to be your destination.

X Marks the Spot

Finding a mentor is imperative to the success of almost any individual, but I especially recommend it to the people in my generation, dubbed Generation X. This group of individuals born between 1962 and 1981 has always faced the scrutiny of the generations that came before us – the Baby Boomers and the Silent Generation.

We have always been characterized as the drive-through, or microwave, generation. We see our desires as "must-haves" – and we must have them *now*. We need to have the latest and greatest toys. We work way too many hours in order to buy a big house in the suburbs and drive a luxury car. Our success is too often measured in personal monetary wealth and stock options.

You see, we have been very fortunate to have become adults during the most prosperous time of the twentieth century. The 1980s and 1990s saw unimaginable growth in technology, pharmaceutical research and real estate. Seemingly overnight, Silicon Valley became a corporate job-seeker's paradise, and the big-payout IPO became an almost universal goal. Though our work ethic has been called into question, most of us are making more at the beginning of our careers than our fathers made at the end of theirs.

Due to this unprecedented corporate growth that has fueled the job market and astronomical salaries, we also have an overabundance of confidence. We consider ourselves great thinkers and extraordinary leaders. We envision ourselves walking in the front door of a company and moving right into the corner office. The reality of Generation X is that we have grown accustomed to living in an era of prosperity. And we have often taken that prosperity for granted. So when the technology bubble burst at the end of the 1990s, the explosion could be felt coast-to-coast. I know many successful individuals who lost their jobs during the "downsizing" that took place at most companies. Most of these individuals could not find work for extended periods of time, even years.

Which brings us to a significant problem, for much of our generation does not know how to deal with adversity. We don't know how to pick ourselves up off the canvas when times are tough. We simply haven't had to experience it before, so we don't have the track record built up to weather this kind of storm. For exactly this reason, I stress finding a mentor, someone who can guide you through the dry spells of your career. If you are truly fortunate, you can find one from the "Silent Generation," the group of people who survived the Depression, lived through World War II, and managed to somehow succeed, shockingly, without the use of a computer or the Internet.

I was very blessed to have a mentor from this generation living in the same house with me while I was growing up. My father's priorities were not a big house or a fancy car. He instead focused on putting food on the table and a roof over our heads, while ensuring that we received a good education. And where did he learn to hold in such high regard these fundamentals of life? By struggling through and overcoming a lifetime of trials.

Strength Born of Adversity

My dad was the eldest of five children. When he was a young boy in the mountains of Calabria, Italy, during the time of the Depression, he was forced to grow up very quickly. At that time, it was customary for the eldest son of each family to go to a nearby monastery to learn from the monks, with the intent of becoming a priest. By following this plan of education, my dad was thoroughly trained in reading, writing, religion and Latin. With the onset of war, however, his journey was interrupted, as it became necessary for everyone to be dismissed from the monastery to go home and help their families. During the months that followed, the monastery was damaged so badly that it became uninhabitable, so, without a monastery to return to at war's end, it quickly became obvious that a path to the priesthood was not in my father's future.

Although the monastery no longer existed, the lessons my father learned there remained etched in his mind. He was filled with the desire to learn more – and the desire to teach. He wanted others to have the opportunity that he had been offered. Unfortunately, however, during the time my father was studying to be a teacher, work became quite scarce in Italy. In order to make enough money for the family to survive, his father and youngest brother had to move to Argentina for three years to become roofers. This left my father with a tremendous responsibility at home – a responsibility that would eventually lead him to drop out of school and move to the United States to find work. Once he settled into a new job across the Atlantic, he began the process of dutifully sending money back to Italy to help support his family there. Even at the very young age of 20, my dad was already determined to make a better life for himself and those he loved.

I can only imagine how he must have felt, journeying to a foreign country, unfamiliar with the language or the culture, and bearing the weight of his family's survival on his shoulders. Now that's adversity! But, as he saw it, he really had only two choices. He could sit back and feel sorry for himself or he could rise to the task at hand, embrace the challenge, and make a difference. Needless to say, he chose the latter.

The Christian writer Mrs. Victor Raymond Edman once wrote,

> "Taken separately, the experiences of life can work harm and not good. Taken together, they make a pattern of

> blessing and strength the likes of which the world does not know."

The pattern my father wove from his experiences yielded tremendous strength. I truly believe that it is often the strength gained through adversity that helps us achieve greatness. It was that strength that drove my father to work a variety of odd jobs – from washing dishes in a restaurant to making paint cans in a factory – in order to ensure the well-being of his family. It was that strength that helped my father choose survival over defeat. And it is that strength that I try to emulate (sometimes more effectively than others!) on my own journey.

If there is a single lesson I would like to leave you with in this chapter, it is this: Simply seek out people of great character, moral strength and work ethic and find ways to follow their footsteps. Walk where the true giants have walked before you. Find people who are willing to share their time and talent with you – and fully embrace the opportunity to learn!

Chapter 2

Develop a Network

Rings on the Water

"The only thing I ever paid full price for was my marriage license."

I cannot tell you how many times I heard that statement while I was growing up. It has always been one of my father's favorite lines, born, I believe, of his desire to periodically remind us of how good a businessman he is! Actually, he wasn't trying to show off, but was simply using an example from his own life experience to awaken in us an early understanding of how the business of our world works. By sharing his personal journey with us over the years, he has taught us countless lessons in the basics of business. Lessons about barter. Lessons about negotiation and compromise. And most importantly, lessons about the value of building a personal network. For even the most "self-made" of professionals have yielded their greatest successes when surrounded by a faithful network of people who trust and respect them for their talents and character.

My father's boyhood home – a small town in southern Italy called Aqua Freda ("cold water" in English) – was situated halfway up a very large mountain. Its real estate amounted to a grand total of seven houses and one general store. Its residents made their living working the land, growing potatoes and wheat, and raising pigs and chickens.

The town's namesake was a large fountain that funneled ice-cold mountain water through two metal pipes protruding from a cement wall. As the town's only source of water, this fountain was the center of activity throughout the day, hosting a constant stream of bucket-toting villagers who would arrive to collect the water they needed in their homes for drinking, cooking, and bathing. A built-in drinking trough for animals and a four-foot-by-four-foot cement basin for washing clothes added to the fountain's importance for townsfolk. Weary travelers making their way up the mountain also found in it a dependable place to quench their thirst and care for their animals.

Hauling this water was a daily task for my father, though only one of many chores that kept him busy in helping to run the family farm. The farm was, first and foremost, the family's food source, with plants and animals yielding a variety of vegetables, wheat, eggs, and meat products. But of equal importance was the fact that their surplus food could be used for barter. And bartering for all that the family needed – the ultimate in negotiation – is how my father's earliest business skills were honed.

Back to Basics

Business in small towns was about the basic survival needs of life – but it was still business. I visited this little town as a child, and one of my most vivid memories was that of the local fisherman, who faithfully emerged from a nearby town every Wednesday morning at six o'clock, as the sun rose upon the land. This man would set up shop and then walk the main road, yelling, "Fresh fish!" for anyone with ears to hear. My dad's family would trade their eggs and other products for those fish. Barter was the name of the game. And if, as a last resort, they had to pay for the fish in a given week, they would never think of paying list price. It just wasn't done. Not unlike today's shrewd corporate moguls, the good businessman in my father's village was always able to negotiate and strike a compromise.

The other lively Aqua Freda business image that sticks with me is the scene of the open market that would descend upon the small town once each year – with its caravan of vendors, loaded down with goods and animals. It was comparable to today's flea markets, in that vendors from all over would bring from the cities their vast array of goods – from shoes to livestock – to sell to the locals. The row of vendors would stretch for more than a half-mile!

Building on the business strength of his tested bartering skills, my dad quickly became a master negotiator with these vendors. And he soon adopted for himself his very first rule of negotiations: He had to be willing to walk away from the deal. It takes courage and a huge dose of self-control, but experience showed that leaving the "negotiating table" almost always resulted in the vendor's coming to his senses and lowering his prices. Over time, my father saved his family a tidy sum through his proficiency in this area. Through these dealings, my father not only learned to stand his ground in negotiations, but also used these opportunities to learn a greater lesson – the need to establish his first network.

For even as a child my dad saw the value of a network. And out of necessity and a desire for success, he built one – comprised of siblings and close friends – to help him get the negotiating done. Standard procedure went something like this: My dad would first approach a vendor alone and pick up a product. After a price was agreed upon, a strategic accomplice would be waiting in the wings, and, at the precise moment the sale was about to be closed, the accomplice would interject and "counsel" my dad that there was a vendor just down the road who actually had the same product with better quality and at lower prices. Thanking the vendor for his time and putting down the product in question, my dad would walk away, inevitably taking no more than five paces before the price of the item would magically be cut in half. This lesson of not settling for a vendor's "fixed" prices is something my father continues to employ fully in his business dealings today. But the greater lesson learned was the value of a trusted network.

Lessons of the Harvest

One of the hardest times of the year for small, rural villages is harvest time. And it is probably during the harvest that having a network is most important to a family's and town's survival. Most of the families in my father's town were far from wealthy, so they could neither own much farm equipment nor afford to hire help. But the annual task was enormous, so for survival at harvest time, family members came out of the woodwork. Everyone from the very oldest in the family to the very youngest had a job. They knew firsthand that there was a small window in which to gather the crops before they went to seed. With the amount of work, however, even with this "all hands on deck" approach, families throughout the village also needed to rely on each other for mutual support.

Plans began to be formed that called for a rotating harvest, in which the villagers joined forces to labor side-by-side and get the job done. In this way, one family's crops would be gathered one week, and another family's crops would be gathered the next. Though small in scale and homespun in flavor, this was truly the ultimate network.

One of the best examples of how this network worked was in the use of an important piece of farm equipment called a *trebia* – a wheat sifter that separates the shaft from the grain. No one in the town could afford to buy one or even rent one on their own, so instead, the villagers would pool their resources to lease the sifter for two weeks. During those two hectic weeks, the sifter would move from farm to farm to help complete the harvesting job throughout the town. When the sifter was at one farm, everyone in the town was there. All the people worked together to create an assembly-line atmosphere that would have made Henry Ford envious. Some people would carry the bundles of wheat to the sifter and hand them to the person who loaded the machine. Others would carry away the shafts packaged by the sifter into nice banded haystacks that would later be used to feed the animals during the winter. Others gathered the grain into large buckets, where it would be stored until the time came for it to be crushed into flour for making bread. Everyone worked together because they had a vested interest. They depended on each other to get everyone's wheat processed in those two weeks or it would cost them all more money. And they depended on each other out of loyalty. This was a true network. A network born out of economic necessity – and a network of the heart.

During one of my summer vacations when I was 15 years old, I actually had the chance to be there during the harvest – and what a life-changing experience it was! While I engaged in some of the hardest work I have ever done in my life, the beauty of an entire town working collaboratively for a common purpose made it also some of the most enjoyable work. It was truly inspiring to see what a group of common people could accomplish when they joined forces and worked together. I often call upon that image when I embark on a new project at work. It really is the business ideal. If I could consistently instill a model in which people worked together for a common purpose and were able to put their individual differences and personal agendas aside for the good of the community, I'd be on the road to fame as a corporate genius. And if, like in my father's small town, the project was always completed on time and within the budget, I'd surely have my pick of companies who wanted me at the helm.

Ripples

Although he never told me this outright, I know with certainty that my dad carried forward that model of an interdependent network later in life when he had the opportunity to open his own business. Over the span of 20 years, my dad owned and operated four different restaurants in a mall in Connecticut. And building and nurturing a network was central to his success.

Picture what happens when a stone is dropped into a pond. After the stone hits the surface, you can see small rings develop around the contact point and slowly move outward. Imagine that you are the stone in the center, and the rings spreading out from you are the individuals affected by your actions. This was the business model that my father employed.

He always believed that the ring closest to him needed to be the strongest. It was the closest to home. The first level of support. The people in direct relationship with him. My father always filled that ring with people he most trusted, the people who most closely shared his values. For him, that ring was made up of his partners and his employees. He believed that if that ring formed a solid foundation for the network, he could then branch out and build with confidence and success.

Having a business in a mall definitely had its advantages. The mall provided not only a steady flow of customers for my father, but also a wealth of other storeowners who shared his same goals and interests. These other owners became the second level of his network – the next ring – because they were all working for a common goal, to make the mall a prosperous place to do business. My dad used this network for many purposes. He would tap into this network to find out if there were any special events planned that would impact the number of people passing through the mall on a given day. For example, one of the busiest days of the year was the day that Santa Claus would land on the roof by helicopter to take up residence in the mall for the remainder of the Christmas season. Equipped with this information, my dad would adjust staffing levels to ensure his ability to effectively meet customer demand.

Networking with other owners had other advantages, as well. When my father saw them come into his restaurant, he would always give them lunch for free. Although most of these owners would insist on paying, they would eventually accept the offer graciously and vow to return the favor whenever my dad was in their stores. This was the barter principle in living color. I would always ask my dad how he could afford to give these people a free lunch. He would explain to me that the entire meal only cost him twenty-five cents, and that even if the person ate there every single day for free, it would cost him less than one hundred dollars for the entire year.

And the benefits certainly outweighed that cost. For he would often take advantage of the 50 to 60 percent discounts offered to him by other storeowners in return for those lunches. He was also the first one they called when merchandise needed to be liquidated to make room for other inventory. As a result, my house was always filled with a host of brand new merchandise, from washers and dryers to sneakers and wide-screen TVs! Every time he would bring home these items, he would first tell us how much it would have cost if he had to pay full price and then have us guess what he actually paid for it. He prided himself on his network, for he held in great value the relationships he gained. These men truly supported each other as colleagues. But most of all, he loved the fact that he was also able to leverage this special network for the benefit of his family.

Just like the rings on the pond continue to expand outward, so did my dad's network. The next level of his network – the third ring – involved all the local professionals that ate at his restaurant almost every day of the week. They were lawyers and bankers, doctors and CEOs. My dad always took the time to know each of his clients and to share a few words with them every time he saw them. Everyone enjoyed his open hospitality, and they always told him that if they could ever be of help, he should not hesitate to call on them.

And so it went. It was this network that helped him meet his doctor, his lawyer, and his insurance agent. It was this network that helped my sisters get job interviews when they outgrew their waitress days and wanted to start careers. (As most of us know, in business it is so often whom you know and not what you know that gets you the initial foot in the door.) And it was this network that enabled him to continue his "bartering ways" for additional benefits. For example, he would always schedule his doctors' appointments around dinnertime, making sure he showed up with a couple of pizzas for everyone in the office. This ensured that he never paid a co-payment for an office visit (again, a pizza that cost him fifty cents to make saved him five dollars) – and certainly cut through any red tape in getting an appointment!

Making a Lasting Impression

The central principle of my dad's business philosophy was simple: Meet as many people as you can, be generous, and leave them with a positive lasting impression. When you do this, you establish a network of support that is powerful in strength and lifelong in scope.

The lessons I have learned from my father's example of surrounding himself with a strong network have served me well throughout my career. Like him, I have worked to nurture a team of supporters that spreads out in concentric circles across the business landscape. My own first level of "rings" consists of the people whom I manage – my own direct reports. I certainly do not hold the title for smartest manager in the world, but I do give myself credit for accepting the simple wisdom that I cannot know everything and cannot be an island. It is this acknowledgement that inspires me to surround myself with bright, dynamic people whom I can trust. These individuals are invaluable to both the given task at hand and to establishing credibility for the department throughout the organization. As with children and their parents, employees so often are seen as a reflection of their manager, and often my staff's trustworthiness, productivity and overall work ethic can make a strong statement about my own credibility and reputation.

Secondly, I make it a point to reach out continually to all of my peers across different departments – the second ring in my network. These individuals help me to answer certain questions that I encounter and provide ideas for creative solutions to problems I might be struggling to overcome. They also share their insight on different ways to run a department. I remember reading once that if you are unable to cultivate a successful culture, find one that is successful and adopt it for your own organization. I am certainly not beyond learning from those who have a team that is flourishing!

I have also learned to develop the third ring of my network – the contacts that I encounter in random situations while doing my job – and in many ways I think that this is the most important circle of all. As a manager, I have a self-imposed metric by which I judge myself: Each and every year, I should wear out two pairs of shoes and go through two boxes of business cards. I manage by being with people – and I try to make connections with as many new people as possible. When I go to conferences, I make sure that everyone I meet walks away with my card. These simple encounters have yielded numerous new client relationships, not to mention a series of great job offers.

The lesson here is another simple one: Develop an active, trusted network and you will reap countless benefits, both personally and professionally. You will never regret the time and energy it takes to do this, for the rewards are vast – and lasting.

Okay, okay, there's one more key lesson to this chapter…Whether in your business or personal life, never, ever pay full price!

Chapter 3

Feed Your Employees

What's On the Menu?

Food courts. A munching paradise for today's mall shoppers. Consumers bask in the convenience of such a wide range of food-related stores being consolidated in one area of a mall. With only a glance over the shoulder, meal- and snack-seekers can see all the food choices at their disposal. And owners of these establishments also reap the benefits, with the area serving as a virtual magnet for hungry shoppers.

What a different dynamic my dad experienced in his work life. Over the span of twenty-five years, I watched him run four different restaurants located in the same mall. However, his restaurants were scattered throughout the mall without rhyme or reason, forcing him – and each of his competitors – to clearly establish a unique offering and reason for being. "More of the same" just wouldn't cut it, as no one was drawn to his restaurants by location alone. In order to be successful, he needed to consistently provide new reasons for clients to actively seek him out.

The same principle of attracting customers in such an environment held true – and continues to hold true today – in the business of attracting employees. Though the job search process is often seen as a sea of individuals hoping to be hired, oftentimes today it is the potential employee who is in the driver's seat. There is such a rich selection of companies today that employers must usually provide compelling reasons for job-seekers to choose them as a potential part of their resume.

The simple solution to the employee attraction dilemma would appear to be higher pay. One can rationalize that those looking for employment will come knocking at the door of the company willing to offer them the most money. And there are plenty of behind-the-scenes bidding wars over the brightest talent that go on in corporate America today. But, while this may work in the short-run, a company approaching things so unilaterally would create a monster. If salary were the only consideration in the employment picture, a salary battle would ensue every time a competitor was willing to pay the employees more money. Companies would experience either constant turnover or would be filing for Chapter 11 status left and right. Either way, the result would be disastrous. It's essential to acknowledge that hiring and retaining employees is about much more than salary alone.

A Well-Fed Staff Is a Happy Staff

After watching my dad interact with his employees over the years, I developed a simple theory about the best way to keep employees satisfied: Feed Them.

When you own a restaurant – especially an Italian restaurant – this theory can first be taken literally. The currency of such a transaction is pizza and pasta. When your employees are hungry, you put something in the oven and give them a meal to eat. Many of the servers that my dad hired were single parents or students that were trying to make ends meet while they went to school. In either case, there was rarely much money to go around. Besides the fact that my dad truly cared for these people and wanted them to be healthy, he also believed that people need to be at full strength in order to do a job right – and that takes nourishment. Waiting tables for ten hours is exhausting, physically-taxing work that requires every ounce of energy a person can muster. Not to mention the fact that, when someone is hungry, serving *other* people food is not the greatest combination for the cheeriest disposition! So my father always made it a priority in his restaurants to ensure that the staff was well-fed at the beginning of each shift.

But he also took this literal feeding a step further. He would make sure his employees took food home with them at the end of the day so that a child or a parent they might be caring for could also have a hot meal. These small gestures of kindness and generosity often lifted a tremendous burden off the shoulders of the staff, and their response was a powerful sense of loyalty to him as an employer, as well as a tremendous love for him as a father figure. Even without these benefits, my dad would have worked like this anyway. He always had a great gift for identifying someone's need and putting a plan in place to fill it. In the business world, however, this approach to life also yielded for him a dedicated, content workforce – a company's greatest asset.

Food for Thought

So what does "feeding" employees mean in the business world today? At its base, it's the same fundamental philosophy that my father employed – taking care of the staff. But feeding the staff today goes well beyond garlic bread and lasagna. Our world is more complicated and our needs are more diverse. How can a manager decide what his employees are hungry for? Part of being a good manager is deciding on the right menu.

Employee Benefits…a modern-day term that tells it like it is. This didn't have a name years ago. It wasn't part of a contract and wasn't written down in an employee manual. But, a key part of the menu that prospective employees are offered when they are considering a job proposal has always been "the rest of the story." The stuff beyond money that rounds out the picture to make a company attractive. The stuff that makes all the difference in both recruitment and retention.

Every company has its standard benefits package – things that everyone on staff has the right to pursue and access. To be competitive in the workplace, this benefits menu needs to be broad and comprehensive. But, to make the situation even more challenging for employers today, most employees not only want a place at the table, but also want their very own meal. There is no "one-size-fits-all" approach that works anymore. People's lives are too complicated. Their needs are too diverse. The world is too difficult. Especially for large departments, with so many "sitting at the table," managers often need to consider adding another leaf!

To Your Health

For many employees, it's all about the health care coverage. Maybe there are financial considerations. Perhaps a spouse is self-employed and has limited, costly health benefits. The employee works part-time just to cover the family's health care costs – often a totally worthy trade-off given today's expensive medical realm. Maybe, instead, there are personal considerations. I know employees who don't care what health plan they are offered as long as their children are able to keep their pediatrician.

What each employee finds important is as varied as the weather, but it's safe to say that, if you don't have a health care plan that is comprehensive enough and addresses such disparate needs, you will find many employees dining at someone else's table.

Training and Advancement

For employees considering continuing education, tuition reimbursement may be a huge benefit. If they can work while they go to school and, in addition, have you to help foot the bill, you may end up with an employee willing to commit four or five solid years to your company before they even think of moving on.

And continuing education is often teamed with the desire to climb the career ladder. If you notice people on your team that are exhibiting leadership qualities, you may want to guide their way into positions of increased responsibility. This vote of confidence and guidance/mentoring will build up your employees and almost certainly help to launch their careers forward.

Some managers are threatened by the thought of helping their subordinates move up, but I don't buy it. My employees' strength is at the heart of my team's strength and the whole department's strength. Someone once told me that good managers always train their departments to the point where they can run without them. This includes training someone to be your eventual replacement. Building future leaders is the responsibility of good managers and a workplace dynamic that is sure to attract and keep many top performers.

But Show Me the Money

I know what some of you are thinking. What I have said up to this point is only an appetizer for most employees. What they want most of all is the meat and potatoes – yes, we're talking *money*. Because, to be perfectly blunt, when someone says, "It's not about the money," they are, in many instances, lying. The test of this principle? Well, would *you* show up every day if they didn't pay you? Doubtful.

But I want to emphasize clearly in black and white: Running a department filled with employees whose <u>only</u> motivation is money is very dangerous. As I said at the beginning of this chapter, if you hire and run an organization based only on the wages you pay, be prepared for a lifetime of turnover and turmoil.

Yes, of course it's important to maintain competitive salary rates in today's economy. Constantly review market data to validate that your salary scale is in line with those of your competitors in the same geographic area. And be attuned to supply and demand. If you are looking for a specific skill set, you may have to "overpay" a candidate in order to secure their services. (This may even result in the need to make a department-wide equity adjustment to retain existing employees.) Be open to creative solutions to the "money part" of the hire. Sign-on bonuses, stock options, and paying for the candidate's moving expenses are just a few of the common approaches.

At the end of the day, no manager in their right mind can afford to be ignorant of or unreasonable about the money stats, but just don't be a *slave* to salary. It really is about so much more.

Can You Relate?

If the mantra in real estate is "location, location, location," the equivalent in business would have to be "relationships, relationships, relationships." And when it comes to the relationships between employees and their managers, study after study has shown that, although an individual may join a company for a variety of reasons, it is, in the end, this crucial connection between employee and manager that will make or break the situation. Both the employee's productivity on the job and longevity at the job are at stake. This is where it all comes together.

Oftentimes, just understanding what is important to employees and offering them the human touch are the things that make relationships work. Give them the recognition they deserve for a job well done. Or the autonomy to make important decisions. Give them flexibility, by allowing them to work out a system to seamlessly blend work and home life. For many employees, their company loyalty is born when they are able to put a child on the school bus in the morning, make a teacher conference or attend a school play. In this age of computer technology, letting an employee work from home when a child is sick is also becoming very popular. It helps the employee – and also keeps a company productive during those long winter months when the flu runs rampant! However you look at it, treating employees as human beings with real lives, desires and struggles will give rise to a more content, productive workforce.

Reward them with trust where it is warranted. And be sure they know that you value their contributions. My dad taught me this lesson when I was about ten years old. Around that time, a ritual started to form between us. When he returned from work at the end of a long day, he would often toss me "the brown paper bag."

On the outside, this bag was a plain paper bag, usually adorned with grease stains or tomato sauce from the day's work. But what was inside the bag was all of the day's cash from my dad's restaurant. My job would be to count all the money in the bag to give him the grand total (being sure, of course to separate all the ones, fives, tens and twenties and arrange them so that all the presidents' faces were facing forward and right side up – important details for dad).

Every night when I finished counting the day's profits, I would give the money back to my dad in a clean paper bag, and he would give me a couple of bucks. I always felt somewhat awkward taking the money because I thought that my reward was just being allowed to help my dad with this important task. But anytime I tried to refuse the payment, my dad would remind me that an honest day's work required an honest day's pay. He told me that he hated this task, but that it was essential to do it to ensure that the next day would start off right. I did good work and I was dependable, and that type of loyalty needed to be rewarded. The money wasn't much, but it showed me that he valued what I did for him.

In my work environment today, the brown paper bag story comes to mind almost daily. I am surrounded by loyal, dedicated people that perform so many tasks that are not glorious but are nevertheless essential to the company's success. When I see that someone is constantly doing his or her job well, I know I need to reward that behavior. When I "toss someone the brown paper bag" and it comes back with the contents all neat and counted, I am sure to extend some form of recognition. Sometimes there is financial reward, but even a simple acknowledgment and words of thanks can be powerful. How you reward them is up to you. Doing it is what matters.

So good relationships are at the heart of employee satisfaction. They take work – but it's work that is worth it. Be prepared to feed well and feed often from a broad menu. Good benefits, advancement opportunities, solid salaries, and human respect are sometimes just a starter list. The more menu options, the greater appeal your organization will have to the prospective "diner." Give them hearty meat and potatoes, but remember to occasionally throw in dessert and coffee.

Chapter 4

Surpass Expectations

The Extra Mile

Companies use many analogies in describing how they go head-to-head with their competition. For some, it's like a high-stakes contest. For others, a battle or a war. Personally, I prefer to think of this competitive challenge as a race. A race in which all competitors must run as hard and fast as possible in order to reach the finish line first, thereby "winning" the customer.

But the most successful companies know that it's actually not about the finish line at all. I know that sounds crazy, for the "finish" usually identifies the winner in our world. But, in today's ultra-competitive marketplace, it is going *beyond* the finish line – going that *extra mile* – that separates the good from the great. Sets the true leaders apart from the pack. *Just* enough *isn't* enough. Customers have certain expectations, and those expectations must not only be met, but often exceeded, or the customers won't be customers for long.

Have you ever gone out to eat at a restaurant and loved the entire experience, only to return a month later to find that the prices have gone up and the portions have shrunk? You went in with a certain expectation, but the restaurant failed to even meet it, let alone exceed it. It will be a long time before you return to that establishment, if ever.

More Than What They Pay For

So how do you deliver more than promised? One important way, of course, is to look at the actual product you are delivering. In many ways, the consumers are in charge of today's marketplace, and they are in a position to demand choices – product selection and breadth. Take a look at the dynamics that have come about with the dramatic changes that have taken place in the "hardware store" business.

Over the years, "mom and pop" hardware stores always served the needs of their customers. If you needed something, you could probably find it there and be satisfied that your purchase would help you to complete whatever project you had undertaken at home. But today, we have "superstores" – and those of us who frequent these places for our home improvement supplies know that these warehouse structures are hardware nirvana. Need a doorknob? You can choose from hundreds of different styles instead of just the two or three you can buy at a smaller shop. How about a faucet? A light fixture? A garden hose? Same deal. In the way of inventory quantity and breadth, these superstores don't just meet the need; they exceed it. They go the extra mile. Of course the level of personal service needs to be addressed to provide the complete package. But if the superstore is also filled with a bunch of highly-informed, eager-to-help employees, it's a recipe for success that goes a long way toward establishing customers for life.

In the healthcare field, the "product" is all about the level of care received by patients, so personal attention and pampering come into play in providing the best. I have seen many examples of patients' receiving better care than they expected. There are institutions that give patients chair massages while they are waiting for oncology treatments. There are others that put Jacuzzi tubs and full-sized guest beds in their maternity rooms in order to make the patients more comfortable. Valet parking and concierge services are becoming commonplace in hospitals. It's just no longer about being "good enough." Patients today are educated consumers who pick and choose where they go to get the best overall healthcare experience. They are by-passing their local hospitals and driving great distances to get the type of healthcare they know they deserve. First and foremost, of course, the medical care itself needs to be top-notch. The staff and their abilities need to meet the highest standards or the other things don't matter much. But, all things being equal in that area, it is the organization that also goes steps further to provide the "rest of the story" that wins the race.

Another way to deliver more than what the customer expects is in the area of quality. I am a firm subscriber to the old adage that "you get what you pay for." And my dad has always asserted that people are willing to pay a little bit more if they know they are getting a better "product." I devote an entire chapter to quality later in the book, so I'll just close this section by reminding you that, whether your product is a physical item or a service provided, build quality in – right from the initial design. In any business, built-in quality means a better product and a better product means a loyal following. Customers will buy the product – maybe time and time again – and be your best public relations team by recommending it to their friends and family.

Service With a Smile

There are probably as many ways to go the extra mile as there are companies, but possibly the most important way has a very familiar name...*customer service.*

So what exactly *is* customer service? We could look up the definition in the dictionary and find some fancy description combining serving, being in touch with customer needs, and quality. But we can't see it. We can't touch it or smell it. Frustrating those of us in business who rely on quantitative analysis to judge "winners" and "losers," customer service isn't something that can be accurately measured. It is one of those "intangibles." There is no definitive dollar value associated with it – no specific income or cost that can be entered in the accounting ledger. No matter how much we wish it, there is no standardized scale to assess why first-time patrons become repeat patrons.

Take the restaurant business, for example. One can measure the number of times a table turns over or how many meals are served per evening. One can measure net profits and inventory amounts. But it is impossible to find a unit of measure that enables us to prove how effectively customers are being served and how satisfied they are with that service.

If you were to hire a suite of top-notch consultants to compare the customer service provided by you and your competitors, they would probably help you develop a customer satisfaction survey that would ask specific questions of your customers – questions aimed at gathering real-life feedback on what is or isn't working in your relationships with the outside world. The results would then be tabulated into a comprehensive database to help you determine what changes needed to be made to improve your level of service. This would certainly be valuable information, but with all the variables in response rates, etc., is it truly an accurate representation of how you are taking care of your clientele? What's a business to do?

Suggestions Anyone?

Many establishments go the route of soliciting on-site written feedback. Have you walked into a restaurant or store that has a suggestion box attached to the wall? Or a stack of cards that ask the important question, "How are we doing?" These are everywhere – at places from hotels to car dealerships. And for a bigger-than-life-sized version of this, how about those "How's my driving?" signs written on the back of tractor trailer trucks all along the interstates?

While these methods are useful and certainly more direct than consultant-driven research, there are still problems related to gathering information in this way. First of all, the experience of the individuals taking time out of their day to fill out these forms has probably been not-so-average. Most likely, their interaction with your organization has been either terrific or horrific! And actually, statistics point out that the complainers will reign here. It has been shown that people who have a great experience share that information with two or three other individuals, while people who have a negative experience share the information with an average of twelve other people! Needless to say, if this holds true, any suggestion box is disproportionately filled with complaints.

Another problem with this type of assessment is that there is no built-in customer feedback loop to show them that their voices have been heard. Once the consumer drops his response in a box, he simply doesn't know what happens to it. For all he knows, it could just get dumped in the trash at the end of the day. Too often there is little or no follow-up with the consumers to let them know that their feedback was received and that changes are being made based on their recommendations. And sometimes the feedback _is_ ignored altogether. How many times have you gone back to a place to "give it another chance" and find that nothing has changed? One sure way to drive your customers away and into the arms of your competitors is to stop listening to their concerns.

Round and Round

I took a customer service class as part of my undergraduate degree. I was so excited to share this information with my dad, so it could help him to start assessing his customers' concerns and increase customer satisfaction in his restaurants. I thought I finally had something I could show *him* about making a difference in the workplace. When I presented my newfound wisdom to him, he just laughed and told me that he would not have been in business for 40 years if he didn't have a clear handle on what his customers wanted and how to keep them satisfied.

I was intrigued by what he had to say. Sure, I knew he had always run successful businesses, but assumed it was for the obvious, tangible reasons like serving up good food in generous portions. I never gave a thought to the fact that my dad may have had a "stealth" customer service plan in operation that kept his customers coming back year after year. I wanted to know exactly what he did to keep his customers satisfied. Well, what he told me should not have been a surprise, for, as with most things in my dad's business approach, it was quite simple. Yet this newest round of "trade secrets" made perfect sense.

First of all, he has always lived by the principle that the best way to find out what customers want is to simply ask them. Not through a suggestion box or response card, but in person. With words. With a smile. Over the course of his restaurant business life, my dad spent countless hours in a process called "rounding." It's simple. Take a few minutes every half hour going from table to table to ask if everything is okay. If something is not right, make sure you fix it right then and there. Give them a free drink or dessert. Bring them a new meal. Whatever is reasonable and fair. Some of these conversations last seconds and others take much longer. Spend as much time as necessary to show the customer that you care and that you're there to make it right. For my dad, not only did this make his customers happy with their experience in his restaurant, but the feedback received from these one-on-one interactions also provided him with an opportunity to look at areas of improvement, and confirm what was going well.

Footsteps of My Father

Over the years, I have used a form of rounding in all of my jobs. When I ran an outpatient laboratory, I could often be found sitting in the waiting room with patients, asking them what they thought of our service. It's amazing what people waiting for a doctor's appointment will share with you! Between the litany of what aches and pains they were suffering, I heard plenty of positive and negative feedback about the service provided by our team. When the news was good, I took that back and shared it with the staff at our department meetings to boost morale. When the feedback was negative, I took that to the staff, as well, and we looked at it as an opportunity to make things better.

Rounding works effectively for internal customers, as well – all those we serve in our management roles *within* the organization, such as our staff, peers and superiors. By rounding, one can interact with the broader team to truly find out what is going on in the department or company. My personal form of internal rounding is delivering the mail. My boss always tells me that I should get someone else to deliver the mail because my time should be spent on "more important things." I always push back, and argue that delivering the mail – which gets me out of my office at least once a day and into the department where much of the work really happens – keeps me attuned to the pulse of the group and also shows employees that we are all in this together. I usually get stopped by at least one employee each day to discuss something that is going on either personally or departmentally. If I don't get approached, I try to seek folks out to do the same thing. The rounding technique keeps me in touch and also sends a message to my staff that I am approachable and do care about what is happening on the front lines and about them as people.

Do-It-Yourself

At the end of the day, I see my father's lessons about customer service adding up to one thing: be involved. Feet-on-the-street involved. Finger-on-the-pulse involved Never let someone else just come in and run your business for you. The minute you delegate responsibility to another individual for the big decisions about your business, you can expect a drop-off in quality. And your being removed from the staff and the customers will cost you dearly. Obviously as a manager you need to delegate tasks to others. No person can do everything, and you also can't be in more than one place at one time. That's not what I mean. What I'm talking about is staying in touch. Take things personally.

Set up a system in which people are held accountable for their actions. Be involved in what's going on around the department or company. Don't adopt an ivory tower management style or you'll find yourself clueless on staff issues or customer needs. Every organization has a different set of dynamics, but you need to thrust yourself onto the frontlines occasionally to assess the climate. Choose the method that's right for you, but get out there and do it. Deliver the mail. Eat in the cafeteria or the break room once a month. Talk to customers. Wait on a table from time to time. Work side-by-side with your employees every once in a while. Maybe even do the tedious tasks in the department like filing or answering phones so you get a flavor of what your employees do. Whatever it is you choose to do, get out where the action is!

If You Build It…

When I think of ways to attract and retain customers, I think of the most famous line from the movie, *Field of Dreams*. The voice tells the main character, "If you build it, they will come."

Yes, certainly build a great product of high quality and value. Build a great organization around you. But also build a business model in which customer service is at the core. Build a business model in which you are personally in touch with both the issues and the victories. Personally in touch with both the customers who put you where you are and the staff that serves them. To do all of this most effectively, take to heart this chapter's central lesson: Build something that goes above and beyond expectations. Go the extra mile. Build all this and they will most definitely come – and, just as importantly, they will keep coming back.

Chapter 5

Leave It at the Office

Shaving Lessons

I am always amazed by the fact that all the technology we have at our fingertips today never helps to shorten the workday. In fact, studies show that the average American is working longer hours today than ever before – and the trend doesn't appear to be changing anytime soon. As a society, we have become slaves to the very technology that "makes us more productive." I'll bet each and every person reading this can remember all too painfully the last time their computer crashed or the last time their cell phone died. We're so dependent on such things that malfunction creates crisis!

I was once working at a major Boston hospital when lightning suddenly blew out the local transformer. Everything went black as night except for the emergency lighting. I remember the darkness, but, most of all, I remember the deafening silence. In the day-to-day pace of office activities, we fail to realize how noisy our work environments have become as we have increasingly been surrounded by electronic devices. Everything has a buzz to it – your computer, the copy machine, the telephone, a co-worker's radio. Funny how workroom acoustics have changed so much in decibels, yet we have somehow managed to block it all out.

With the silence of that blackout came the feeling of helplessness. At first, everyone was mulling around, lost as to what they should do. Then a slight panic set in, as people began to feel cut-off from the outside world. I don't think anyone felt like they were in danger. The fear was more related to the impact this loss of power would have on their technology tools. Concerns were centered on, "What if someone tries to e-mail me?" and "How do I add this row of numbers without my Excel spreadsheet?" It's amazing, but we have forgotten that we have done things for years without sophisticated technology, and that we actually did all learn to add numbers without the assistance of a calculator!

An Office That Never Sleeps

Personally, I can't imagine my life without technology. It is so all-encompassing that it defines how we do nearly everything. And it does increase both the types of things we are able to do and how quickly we can do them. Yes, technology is a blessing, but it also can make our lives a lot more difficult.

Take those of us who work in a moderately complex work environment. The day usually starts off by checking voice mails and e-mails remotely from home. Yes, with this advent of "productivity tools," we can already be at work even before we take a shower or have breakfast. (Some people even set an alarm to awaken them for work in the wee hours of the morning while the rest of the house is still asleep. They justify that this is their time of peak productivity!) After "catching up," it's time to jump in the shower – not only to clean up, but also to rehearse that day's big presentation.

Fast-forward a little bit to the post-shower-but-still-at-home phase of readiness. After getting dressed, we strap on a utility belt that would make Batman proud. It's equipped with a pager and a cell phone so that everyone who depends on us – and many who don't – will know where we are at all times. Then toss a PDA in the coat pocket so that we always know *ourselves* where we're supposed to be. This baby beeps at us before every meeting to ensure we make the next rotation on the schedule in a timely fashion.

Fast-forward a little more and we are now in the car – in the garage anyway. Before starting the car, we put in our earpiece so we can use our mobile phone to do business while we are on our way to work. Wouldn't want to waste any precious time "just driving." We check the traffic report to make sure we will have the quickest commute possible. Amazingly enough, we have already put in more than an hour's work and we haven't even left our driveways yet.

After a productive commute, we pull into the company parking lot, ready to "start" our day. Most of you know how the day goes. Twelve hours of meetings, phone calls and presentations, and then we can finally leave the office. But don't be fooled – leaving the office usually does not signal the end of the day anymore. Don't forget to grab the laptop in order to work on some miscellaneous stuff at night while watching the evening news.

So now we're in the car again for the reverse commute home. As with the morning drive, our commute home has become as complex as a NASA shuttle launch. Earpiece? Check! Traffic report? Check! Beeper switched from silent to audible alarm? Check! "Average worker, you are clear for take-off. Have a safe ride home." Once we're convinced we have picked the quickest way home, we break out the PDA once again and record miscellaneous ideas that we don't want to risk forgetting.

For some of us, the evening commute doesn't always lead directly home. Often, we find ourselves making pit stops at the local drive-through for a quick bite to eat. Or if it *is* a straight shot home for a nice home-cooked meal, it's unfortunately too commonplace that the once-delicious meal was cooked four hours ago and sits on a plate covered in plastic wrap waiting to be microwaved. Of course by that time, there's the added bonus that there's no one to enjoy the meal with us. It's probably a school night, and the kids are in their final approach to bedtime. Not too healthy for the family, but we really don't have time for small talk anyway – we have work to do!

After we eat some version of dinner and comb over important documents for a few hours, we decide to call it a night – but not before checking voice mail and e-mail one final time. Never know what important stuff might have gone down in the last couple of hours. Before turning out the light, we make sure the pager and cell phone are right beside the bed because there might be a situation in the middle of the night that would require our attention.

Anthony Rino

Exit Technology, Enter Dad's Approach

Although I occasionally find myself getting caught up in some of these bad behaviors born of "too much of a good thing," I also return to my father's example often. What would he do in this situation? Just imagining this always provides me with my best laugh of the day because, well, to put it bluntly, my dad is the most technologically illiterate person I know.

He is the only adult I know who does not even have a car, let alone an answering machine, cell phone, ATM card, email address or calculator. When I question him about how he lives without these "necessities," his answers are brief but to the point. "Why do I need a car when I can take the bus?" "I don't need an answering machine. If people want to talk to me, they can call me when I am at home." Cell phone, (See answering machine). ATM card, "What, banks don't have tellers anymore?" As far as the calculator goes, my dad, quite simply, has always done the math in his head. In the forty years he ran a business, he never used a calculator or a cash register. Okay, I stand corrected; he did use a cash register. But used only one button on the register – the one that opened the drawer. It didn't matter how big or small your order was. He did the math in his head, including the tax. My dad felt that, since he had been adding numbers long before the calculator was invented, why on earth mess with what worked.

So the technology comparison is a big "N/A" on the chart, but what did my dad teach me about the long work hours? He first taught me that anything worth doing right will, in fact, take much of your time. But being very dedicated to your work – and the long hours this often requires – does not need to mean the ruthless invasion of life at home.

Believe me, my dad was no stranger to long hours. You'll see later in this book that his work schedule was, in fact, not a healthy aspect of his life. He worked long and hard – to a fault. But he also believed that one's hours need to be efficiently separated – work was work and home was home. To help himself manage the transitions between the two, he always had his morning routine and his evening routine.

His morning routine was a shower and then a shave. Yes, those shaves were a prelude to the workday, but also a part of family time. There were times when he would put shaving cream on his face and then put some on mine. While I waited patiently, he would unscrew the top of a razor to remove the blade and hand that one to me to "shave" alongside him. We talked about a lot of things, but none of them were ever about work. After the shave, it was time for a breakfast of toast and tea. No drive-through. No grabbing a quick bite at the office. A good breakfast at home was the best way to start the day off right.

Routine for a New Generation

As much as I loved that early morning time we had together, today I cherish those early lessons even more. In fact, I believe in his philosophy so much that I have started my own morning rituals. My commute to the office is usually accompanied by a book on tape or morning prayer. But before I even get behind the wheel, I live out my most important morning ritual – when I wait with my children and put them safely on the school bus. This time – and the talks we share during it – is by far the best part of my morning. Any of you who have seven-year-old and five-year-old children can easily imagine what it's like – and how diverse the conversation can be. "Daddy, how many more days are there until Christmas?" "Why can't I pick up bird feathers?" "Why are school buses yellow?" Although I sometimes can't make the breakfast-at-home goal a reality, the morning "school bus talks" inevitably put me in the right frame of mind to start my day and give me perspective for the inevitable stresses of the office.

Time to Wind Down

For any business person, the end of the day often brings as many challenges as the beginning of the day, so my dad was devoted to an evening routine, as well. If it was still light when he got home, he would usually head into the yard and tend to his garden for a while. He told me once that this close-to-the-earth labor helped him decompress from even the most hectic of days. He would pick tomatoes, tie up some drooping plants or spend a little time just watering the dry soil. All of these activities would make the memories of a hard day fade away. I did notice that, once my dad came in after gardening, he was almost always relaxed and calm. Home was then for family.

Since having a morning routine is working out so well for me and my family, I recently started my own evening routine, as well. The gardening theme is a consistent one – and let's just say that my neighbors love my tomatoes!

Most importantly, however, my evening routine is anchored by time with my family. Working far fewer hours than my dad, this is even more central to my own experience. For those of you with family at home, I'm convinced that this one is non-negotiable – and the most valuable thing you'll do all day. Dinner together is so important – but even if that can't be a reality at times, still be sure to take the time to collect a whole day's worth of hugs and kisses. Nothing helps you leave the workday behind you like two arms squeezing you with all their might.

Lesson? When it comes to your life, there is no such thing as a "Do-Over." Start work when you get there, not before. Leave work at work. (I guarantee it will be waiting there the next morning when you get back.) Just because you have the *ability* to make your world your office, resist the temptation to do so – and enjoy the beauty of having a *life*.

Chapter 6

Get in the Trenches

The Dishwasher

The dictionary defines a manager as a person who is in charge of business affairs. But all too often, managers have a faulty interpretation of what "in charge" denotes in the workplace. I don't hold out a lot of long-term hope for organizations with managers who think being in charge means that certain duties in the department are beneath them. It's not sound thinking, and it does not help to build a healthy organization. Unfortunately, most of us have been there at some point in our careers – often the first time we become a manager or supervisor. It's easy to have the grave misconception that we have just been infused with great power, when in reality what has been given to us is great responsibility.

Many first-time managers struggle with their new roles. And this is especially complicated when a manager is chosen from within the department – a so-called "internal" candidate. At face value, this looks like an ideal plan – to hire someone who has "been there in the trenches" to lead the troops. But the fact that one day you're somebody's co-worker and the next day you are his or her supervisor often, with good reason, can put all sorts of strain on relationships. Spending so much time coming up to speed on new responsibilities, the new manager can get easily overwhelmed, quickly forget the stresses of their last job, and find it impossible to sympathize with the staff's struggles. The tuned-in staff sees this immediately, creating instant animosity, so the manager starts to resent the new job completely and the entire place starts to fall apart!

There are many wonderful internal candidates ready for management promotions, but companies need to be more aware that being the best "front line" worker does not *always* translate into being the best leader. And even great program leaders are not necessarily great people leaders. In the end, it is the blending of a person's natural gifts with solid management training that makes this work. Whether new managers come from within the company or outside it, find the people with leadership potential, teach them, and give them the tools and guidance to grow.

All Hands on Deck

One problem my dad has never had is that of understanding the employees' perspective. As boss, he has never felt he was "above it all." No head swelled with false self-importance for him. Management, in my dad's eyes, implies that you know everything about your operation – and that includes knowing every job in it. To be successful, you not only have to know every job, but also need to be prepared to *do* them – at any time – in order to keep up with production. There can be no job that you consider beneath you or unworthy of your time and effort.

My dad asked me once who I thought the most important person in his restaurant was. I naturally said that he was the most important. After all, he was the owner. He just laughed and said to try again. I thought about it a bit longer this time, and told him that it must be the chef – the one who makes all those delicious meals that keep people coming back for more. But I could tell from my dad's expression that he was not thinking of the chef either. Baffled, I continued to think about the operation, and then took a new guess – the waiters and waitresses. All the delicious, hot food in the world would never get to the customers' mouths if these folks didn't take their orders and carry the plates from the kitchen. Still a shake of the head from my dad. Nope, not them. I finally gave up on this game, and asked him who it was. "The dishwasher," was his answer. Not exactly at the top of my mind.

He then went on to explain that business in a restaurant, of course, is based on turnover – getting people in and out. Well, central to that turnover is the fact that you must be sure to have enough clean plates at all times in order to keep up with the demand from the people at the tables. If the dishwasher were to call in sick and no one else could do the job, you might as well close your doors because you would eventually run out of clean plates. Without clean plates you could not serve food. End of story.

I thought about it for a while and, figuring this actually must happen from time-to-time, asked him how he handles it when the dishwasher *does* call in sick or take a vacation. "That's easy," he said. "I become the dishwasher. And, by the way, I also become the waiter or the cook or whomever is not in on any given day." Sometimes this would involve doing these roles even when someone was not missing, but just overloaded with work. In a healthy workplace, people fill in for each other, help each other out. And a good manager knows that it doesn't work to take the attitude of being "above" all of this. In order to manage a successful department, managers need to get into the mix sometimes. Be in the trenches. Get their hands dirty. Help the organization to realize that everyone is in this together. When one of the areas fails, then everyone fails. If a customer leaves disappointed, it's because the group failed to meet that customer's needs. When people are willing to put their titles aside and accept the fact they may have to do some things that are not in their job description, everyone benefits. The organization can flourish, and the customers are happy.

Sharing the Load in Today's Workplace

I think this philosophy translates well to almost all businesses. Obviously there are many jobs that require a certain technical or clinical skill set, a special license, or a certain level of educational training. It is not realistic to think that in all cases, a manager can swoop right in and go about the jobs of any staff member. However, that does not minimize the fact that every individual in the department plays a role that is vital to the department's success.

For example, regardless of our job we are all responsible for how clean our department is. If we see trash on the floor we should pick it up – simple as that. Walking right by sends the wrong message to your staff – a message that the task is beneath you and that the responsibility of keeping the place clean clearly falls on someone else's shoulders. The message we should be sending is that we are all in this together and that one job is just as important as another.

In the corporate world where competition and market share often drive our operations, we rarely take the time to recognize the vital people that surround us on a daily basis. I actually sat down one day and asked myself the question my dad had asked me. Who was the most important person in my own department? I had a very difficult time deciding, but I did have a revelation. I knew who the least important person in the room was at that moment – me! You see, while I was sitting there making my observations, everyone else was very busy going about their work. In a similar way, when I go off to meetings, everyone else is "back at the ranch" giving their all to make sure things keep running. Without that dedication and hard work at each and every job in the group, I could be a genius – and the group would still fail to live up to its potential.

Another way to look at this is through, forgive me, a football analogy. The secretaries that answer the phones are our first line of defense. If they do not answer the phone courteously or if they fail to answer the caller's questions, they risk losing the customer almost before the play has begun. I, on the other hand, am the free safety. In football, the free safety sits farther back than anyone else. If the rest of the defense fails, the free safety is the last person standing between the offensive player and the end zone. If everything goes well, the free safety isn't even close to making a play. As the manager, I am inevitably the fielder of complaints that are difficult to address. These complaints eventually come my way when there was some kind of breakdown in service between the department "front line" and the customer. But most problems never make it that far. Just like a free safety with a great defensive team, having the right people in front of me is essential.

I encourage every manager out there to take a look at your own department – I mean closely – to truly find out what it is that every single individual does. Too often as managers we *think* we know how the job responsibilities shake out, but we really don't have that insight until we start talking to people. Talk to the people who answer the phone, open the mail, and do the typing. And find out how you can make their jobs easier.

Are there systems in place that are creating unnecessary duplication of efforts? Can the work be streamlined? Are there certain tasks that are not even necessary at all? In a conversation with one of my employees, I found out that she spent two hours per day separating lab reports to go to the hospital floors. I asked why we continued to do this when we had invested in a computerized access system that allowed doctors to receive their patient's results in real-time via the computer. Well, it turned out that a couple of doctors had continued to request the paper reports because they had a real aversion to computers. After discussing this with hospital administration and offering better training for the medical staff, we were able to eliminate this practice all together. Because of a ten-minute conversation, I was able to free up two hours of an individual's time so that she could dedicate herself to other, more essential and rewarding tasks. This clearly created a better job situation for her and a mutual respect between us.

If there is one recurring complaint from first-time managers, it is that their staff does not respect them. Well, there are really two ways to get respect. You can earn it or demand it. I assure you that earning it makes life a whole lot easier! But how do you earn the respect of your staff? That's actually what this entire chapter has been about. It's all tied together, and it's so simple…

1. Learn what your employees do. Only when you do this can you provide them with the proper orientation, training and resources to be successful.

2. Pitch in when they need you. Don't be afraid to get your hands dirty.

3. Be a good listener. Don't try to solve problems before the employee has a chance to finish explaining what's wrong.

4. Be visible. Nobody likes managers who lock themselves in their offices.

5. Respect *them* first. The most important rule of earning someone's respect is to show respect in return. To show respect, you need to value the work they do. Understand what value they bring to your department and celebrate their achievements. Acknowledge them when they do things well. Give

them feedback constructively when things could have gone better. No matter what you have read about keeping your distance as a manager, don't be afraid to care about your staff. They are not merely a name on a timesheet – someone identified only by title or job function.

The lesson here is one of respect, understanding, and willingness to be a hands-on part of solutions at times. Successful managers do not build imaginary walls between themselves and their staffs. On the contrary, they build bridges. Never forget, if your dishes are dirty and there is no one willing to clean them, you might as well just close up shop.

Chapter 7

Choose Wisely – You Get What You Pay For

Good Shoes

To be successful, my dad told me long ago, you need a good pair of shoes. Frankly, even though I nodded politely when he said it, I didn't really have the slightest clue about what that meant. So I made the assumption at the time that he was speaking literally. After all, for a person who spent as much time on his feet as he did, it made sense that a solid, quality pair of shoes would be essential.

As with many of the exchanges we had while I was a young boy, I asked him later as an adult what he had meant by the "good shoe story." Was I ever surprised to hear the wisdom behind the simple comment! He explained that most new shoes – whether of cheap or quality construction – look the same on the shelf or in the box. They might even feel the same for the first few weeks' wearing them. The problem is that those first few weeks are just the trial phase. Any shoe can feel good and look good. But how will the shoe hold up over time? Will it keep its support? Will it be attractive and comfortable after it gets wet a few times? A quality shoe will stand the test, but a cheaply-made one will fall apart under the stress and strain of daily life.

The shoe story never crossed my mind again until I got to graduate school and heard a story about W. Edwards Deming. During a lecture, someone commented that they really liked the shoes Deming was wearing, and went on to ask him how much they cost. Deming's reply was, "I don't know. I'm not done wearing them yet."

This story may sound a bit enigmatic, but, in light of my dad's earlier lesson on quality, it made perfect sense to me. You see, the cost of a pair of shoes is not merely what you pay for them, but also what you get out of them. If Deming's shoes looked good, but didn't have the quality to stand the test of time, he'd only get a few months of use out of his shoes, and the true cost would be great. If, however, he were able to get several years of use out of his shoes, the cost, in the end, would be modest. Makes sense when you look at it that way, doesn't it?

Let's face it, at the point of purchase, items of varying quality may not look any different – and those of better quality often cost a bit more, but what's the cost in the end? In life, you truly get what you pay for.

"Shopping" for Employees

Managers charged with the huge responsibility of interviewing employee candidates understand that the search for good staff members is actually a lot like shopping for a good pair of shoes. (Okay, we'll put aside the fact that, with the rate at which people change jobs today, my shoes will probably outlast most of my new hires!)

If we're not careful, we can easily be fooled by outward appearances. Many potential employees look similar "on the shelf or in the box." Most people, if they really want a job, show up for an interview looking very polished – with business clothes clean and pressed, hair perfectly-coiffed, nails expertly trimmed and breath minty fresh. Not too many people show up looking like disorganized slobs. But they can be just like those shoes that look great, but fall apart after a month. If we only hired people based on appearance, I can only imagine what kind of staff would result.

Bear with me as I take the shoe analogy even further. Let's look at the timing of the "purchase cycle." Ask most people how long it takes them to buy a pair of shoes and they probably will say it takes less than an hour – a very short amount of time. (Please note that this analogy only works if we are talking about the average person buying an average pair of shoes. The parallel falls apart if the complicating factors of matching handbag or outfit come into play. That search could take weeks!)

In the "people-shopping business," the interview itself is set up to gain the most amount of information in the shortest amount of time. As with the shoe purchase, it's rare to dedicate more than a single hour to interview any candidate. With this short cycle, we might be overlooking something important or overemphasizing something insignificant. You wouldn't buy shoes without trying them on, and you shouldn't hire or rule out potential employees without doing the same. Give them a chance to show their quality.

We all do this timeless routine with shoes. We take that little jaunt back and forth in the shoe store, stopping to see what the shoe looks like in those little floor mirrors designed to only show you from the calf down. We have to really check them out to make a sound purchase. The same applies to a candidate. How many times do we eliminate candidates by just looking at their resume? Just one little peek and we make a potentially hasty decision about whether they are "in" or "out." We can also be swayed by "brand identity." When buying shoes, we sometimes look for a certain model or brand with which we may have had success in the past. Something that gives us that mental "stamp of approval" at the outset. When hiring a potential employee, these brands could be things like an MBA or a degree from a prestigious college or university. While this can be a good *start* in an assessment, unfortunately, some managers can't get past the "brand," and most times won't hire or even interview an individual who does not possess these qualities.

It may sound like I'm suggesting you spend time you surely don't have as a manager – but it's time well-spent. You don't even have to have a candidate in for a complete interview, but at least have a discussion on the phone. The person may show some potential, and you can then schedule a face-to-face meeting. An initial phone interview has another benefit, as well. It allows you to focus on the candidate's responses to your questions and not be distracted by appearances. Sometimes in face-to-face meetings, managers have a tendency to eliminate a candidate within the first few minutes of an interview because they focus on a perceived flaw the individual has. The interview may last an hour, but in reality it ended after the first five minutes.

I'll end the shoe analogy the way I began – by reminding you that you do get what you pay for. When it comes to product, resist the urge to cut corners. Doing so may not be immediately apparent to your customers, but it will eventually catch up to you. Never forget that customers have many choices out there. Take pride in the product you are putting on the market and stand behind it. Loyal customers will be your reward.

As for people, just like Deming said about not knowing the cost of a pair of shoes until you are finished wearing them, the same can be said for a new hire. Companies spend such a tremendous amount of money interviewing and training their employees to the company culture, but you don't really know what a new employee will cost you until they become a former employee. An employee that does not make it past their 90-day probation period costs a company a bundle. But an employee that goes on to have a long and productive career is like a good pair of shoes – worth every penny. Quality counts. Spend the time to find the best that you can, and make the investment.

Chapter 8

Do What You Love

The Photograph

I keep an old photograph of my dad on my refrigerator at home. The picture was taken when my dad was about 19 years old, right before he left Italy for the United States. I love this particular picture because it was taken at a time of incredible promise in his life. A time when he had his whole life ahead of him.

This photo of a young man without any wrinkles and a full head of black hair always inspires me to wonder what was going through his mind at that time. It makes me want to ask him, "What were your dreams? What were some of your favorite things to do in life? What did you want to achieve?" Some people might find it odd that I ask rhetorical questions to a picture that can't respond instead of picking up the phone and asking my dad these same questions. But I find that talking to my dad about that time in his life is difficult for him.

Dad was always the strong, silent type. A man of few words, he let his actions speak for him. But even when we did talk, the more distant topics of school and politics were most often the focus of the discussion. Personal reflection just didn't happen. My dad has had a lifetime surrounded by people who love him, and for that I know he is truly grateful. But he has led a hard life, and has chosen to accept it quietly.

The strapping, young 19-year-old on my fridge is now a 73-year-old man who has labored ceaselessly. The full head of hair is now all gray and grows only on the sides of his head. The strong features of his face are now masked by the wrinkles that come with years of hard work. Yes, his appearance has certainly changed over the years, but what is inside him – what truly makes him who he is – will never change.

Reasons to Get Up in the Morning

Over the years, I came to realize that there were really three key things that got my dad excited – three things that motivated him to get out of bed and dive into each day: work and being a good provider for his family, cooking, and, well, if you must know, professional wrestling.

The cooking part – easy to see, since restaurants were his field of expertise. Quite simply, he has always loved to witness the enjoyment people get from eating a well-prepared, delicious meal.

I'll get back to the work/providing theme because, of course, it's the cornerstone of this entire book. But let me cut to the chase on the wrestling thing because I'm sure you're so curious about this oddity that you won't concentrate on anything else I write here until I explain further!

I remember the first time I actually saw my dad let his guard down. In that brief moment, we made a special connection. In high school, I worked as a waiter in a local restaurant, and I would work all the weekend shifts. The Saturday shift usually went past 11 p.m., and, by the time everything was cleaned up, I would return home around midnight. My first stop was always the kitchen – to heat up some leftovers that I could eat while watching some TV and unwinding from the long night at work.

One night I came home and my dad was still awake. I came in to find him in front of the television, watching, of all things, wrestling. I'm not talking Olympic wrestling. I'm talking the totally phony spectacle of men in tights and gaudy outfits screaming challenges at each other to rile up the crowd. Bad theater, I believe it would be more aptly named. As I ate my dinner that night, I was amazed to witness my dad periodically get up, pace the floor, and actually shake his fists at the TV to cheer on his favorite contender. I reminded him that this was fake – purely a show with a predetermined outcome. He said he knew that the whole thing was an act, but that didn't stop him for a second from jumping up out of his seat during the very next match to yell at the referee about something illegal happening in the ring. For the first time in my life, I got a glimpse of something that my dad really enjoyed.

After that night, my dad and I had a standing date every Saturday. I would come home at midnight, and he would have the TV already on and have a plate set for me with my dinner so I wouldn't have to miss any of the action. Over two years, there were very few Saturday nights that we didn't spend watching wrestling together. This farce of entertainment was an opportunity for me to enjoy some time with my dad. There was no talk of business or politics or school – and I did notice that his attention gradually grew to be more focused on our personal conversations. I believe he started to truly enjoy that time we spent together – even more than the crazy programming. It was over those two years that I actually got to know my dad as a person – not just someone who lived in the house with us. I was blessed to gain insight into this and other interests – the things he was passionate about. Some of them were predictable, and some – case in point – totally unexpected.

So, back to dad's love of work. I have never before or since known anyone with a comparable work ethic. Now "retired," he still manages to hold down two part-time jobs and works sixty hours per week. If you ask him why he does that, he will tell you quite simply that he loves to work. I have to admit, I really struggle with the idea of work as such a big motivator in someone's life. For him, though, while a lot of the work he did was very physical and took its toll on him over the years, he has always truly enjoyed it – but for totally different reasons than most people today.

A common list of "likes" for the majority of today's workforce would include such things as good salary, flexible schedule, or short commute. But not for dad. Topping his list is relationships – the fact that work gives him an opportunity to meet new people every day. He believes that everyone has a story to tell, if we only take the time to listen.

Also on his list is the fact that he has been able to provide for people one of the basic needs of this world – feeding them. Growing up in an Italian family, I often wondered why we had a living room in our house at all, as ninety percent of the action took place in the kitchen. Even now, when my wife and I entertain, our kitchen is always the gathering place, and the conversations always seem to go better when there is plenty of food and wine to go around. My dad always saw his restaurants as opportunities to bring people together and pamper them with good food, just as you would do in your own home.

What his priorities and "list of likes" show me is that, when you love what you do at work, it really doesn't seem like work at all. That's the secret. Because without the love of what you do, it really is just work.

From "Retirement" to "Part-Time"

When I was in college, the mall where my dad had his restaurant was closing its doors after twenty years. There were financial incentives to help relocate some of the businesses, but my dad decided instead to take the buyout of his lease and retire. I wasn't there to witness it, but my mom tells me that retirement simply did not agree with my dad. In fact, he began to drive her crazy! He just was not happy, so he decided to take a "part-time" job working at the concession stand at the local zoo. I loosely use the term "part-time" because it was actually a forty-hour-per-week commitment. I guess when you put in sixty-hour weeks over a forty-year career, forty hours must feel like part time. The job was pretty simple – cooking hamburgers and hot dogs for the zoo patrons. And he loved it!

He called me one day to tell me that he had missed a day of work because he was sick. I immediately asked him if it was serious because in my lifetime, I can probably count on one hand the number of days he has called in sick. It just doesn't happen. He assured me he was fine and that it was just a cold, so I was confused about why he would then go out of his way to call me about this. Well, as it turns out, it wasn't the fact that he had called in sick that got my dad all excited, but the fact that they actually paid him for that day. When I asked him why he was so surprised, his response was, "You mean you *knew* about this?" It was like the whole concept of benefits and sick time was an underground conspiracy against people who ran their own businesses. Never in a million years did I guess that my dad was completely unaware of the benefits associated with a job that all of us in corporate America take for granted. Most of us see our benefits package as an entitlement, failing to recognize that there are individuals all over the place out there who don't share in the privilege. For him, the joy of the work itself has always been a "benefit."

It wasn't long after the zoo job took hold that my dad took another part-time job in a pizza place. I guess once a pizza guy, always a pizza guy. This was only three nights per week, for a total of twenty hours per week. For those of you keeping track, this brought my dad's "part-time" job grand total to sixty hours per week. Some retirement! I recently asked him why he doesn't retire for good, for he doesn't need the money. He explained that he isn't doing it for the money, but because he truly loves what he is doing. For salary does not necessarily equate to the level of success you have reached. My dad can now go to work, cook, talk to a bunch of people and then go home. He no longer has to worry about keeping the books or ordering from vendors. Instead, he can focus on the parts of his job that he loves the most.

The whole thing makes me feel a little guilty because, in all honesty, there are times when I am counting the days until I can retire. When I told my dad that I look forward to that big day, he told me that once you get to a point where you no longer have to work, your perspective on work changes. And when you love what you do, it's not really work at all.

Maybe that's an extreme statement, and work will always seem like work to us, but surely we can all find things that we enjoy about our jobs. It's just all in how you look at things. On my dad's lunch hour at the zoo, for example, he often walks through the botanical gardens and picks up seeds that have fallen to the ground – seeds he then takes home to plant in his own garden. I'll tell you, sometimes I don't recognize the house I grew up in because it has taken on such a tropical appearance with those exotic plants growing everywhere! The point is, he found something that was enjoyable and important to him, right in his work environment.

So What Do You Love?

As managers, we need to help employees recognize what it is that they like about their jobs – and what it is that we like about our own. Personally, I love the teaching and the coaching aspect of my job. I love spending time training staff members and teaching supervisors how to formulate a budget or interview a potential candidate for the first time. I enjoy the time itself, and I usually come away from these experiences more enriched for having shown someone a new skill. It's like they say, "Give a man a fish and he eats for a day; Teach a man to fish and he eats for a lifetime." As managers, we can have a tendency to swoop in and "fix" problems. But if we don't take the time to teach people how to fix them themselves, those same problems will recur. I like to teach, and I take every opportunity to do so with my staff – both for their benefit and mine.

If there is nothing about a job that you love and a career change is not in the cards, I would suggest teaming up your income-earning career with some other rewarding work of your choosing. Volunteering, running for public office, or sitting on a committee that is involved in work that really interests you are just three such suggestions. Three years ago I actually took on a part-time job – ironic because I criticized my dad for doing the same – when I was asked by a friend to help teach a Quality Management class at the university where I had received my undergraduate degree. Although the pay was minimal, the experience was extraordinary. And as I said earlier, teaching is one of my passions. I just love the fact that I can share my knowledge and experience with people and help them achieve their own life goals. In addition to teaching at the university level, I also teach high school religious education. If you're keeping track, yes, I now have two part-time jobs, just like dad. Jobs for which the rewards are certainly not monetary, but priceless nevertheless.

So determine what inspires you to do great work – what it is about your job that you find rewarding. If you haven't done so in a while, take a walk around your organization and find out what interesting work is going on right in your own department. You may be amazed at the things that are happening and may even want to be a part of them. Also take a walk through your broader organization's "botanical garden." Pick up the interesting "seeds" and bring them back to your department to see what grows.

Most of all, *never* compromise on this one fact: Do what you love. My 19-year-old dad in the photo on my refrigerator knew this wisdom even then. It is only when we love what we do that it stops being work and truly becomes an answer to a calling – a vocation for life.

Chapter 9

Don't Let Your Job Become What You Are

Daddy's Shirts

In an earlier chapter, I commented that in life there is no such thing as a "Do-Over." And with that thought tucked in the back of my mind, I set out to write this book's last and most difficult chapter. Why difficult? Well, up to this point, every management lesson I have shared with you was inspired by a *positive* experience with my father. I've explored how his pure, straightforward, honest approach to business and life is a model that today's companies would do well to emulate.

But there was one more thing I learned through his guidance – and it's something I'm working hard *not* to emulate in my own life. For my dad, I believe, allowed himself to be consumed by his job.

Unlike the other lessons, so often born of the "words of wisdom" my practical father shared with me over the years, this lesson was not one I learned through words. My dad never spoke words to me on this subject – because he never had to. I instinctively learned this final lesson by watching him over the years. He has always been the hardest worker I know, and, as I said earlier, he taught me the important lesson of "leaving it at the office." The problem was that he didn't leave the office much!

Working to that extent is not without price. And unfortunately the price can be exorbitant. A price that you don't even realize you are paying until you're looking at your career through the rearview mirror years later.

You see, I didn't have a "normal" childhood (but then again, what does that mean anyway?). It was a great one, though, for I had two loving parents. I am grateful for both their love and how they provided for me and my sisters. But I was a mall rat – someone who spends extraordinary amounts of time hanging out at the mall. No, I was nothing like today's mall rats, who are dropped off at the mall for no apparent reason, only to saunter around aimlessly in their baggy pants and midriff shirts, with cell phones surgically attached to their ears. In my case, I was at the mall because, quite simply, that's where my whole family was. My dad ran the restaurant, while my mom cooked in the kitchen and both of my older sisters waited on tables. I was the little kid taking naps in the back room on 100-pound bags of flour. Most of the time I used my time to help out in the kitchen to the best of my ability. At first it was washing dishes or sweeping floors, which later led to mixing the dough or making the sauce. The work was tough, but I actually enjoyed it. I got to spend the day with my entire family and I felt very connected to be in a family business together. When I was at the restaurant, I got to spend a lot of time working side-by-side with my dad, and that was time I treasured. Working at the restaurant with my family gave me some of the earliest and best memories I have to this day.

So it wasn't until I was older that I realized that my relationship with my dad was different than that of most fathers and sons. For dad and I never played catch, and never played a game of hide and seek. I have never seen my father dance, not even at my wedding. I don't remember ever taking a family vacation after the age of eight. And he never once came to see me play football. When I was in high school, football was my life. Before each game I would look up in the stands, hoping that would be the game that would be different. Forty-one games over a four-year career, and never did he once find the time to see me play. I share these experiences with you not to evoke sympathy, but to illustrate what sacrifices are made by someone who allows himself to be consumed by work. Whenever there was an important event in my life while I was growing up, it always seemed that my dad had to work. I know running a business takes a lot of time but at the end of the day you have to ask yourself, "Is it worth it?"

Footsteps of My Father

Then one day it hit me. While it upset me a great deal that my father never came to watch me play football, it was, in fact, *he* who was missing out most of all. He was missing out on *my* life. I wasn't missing out on his. If there was anyone who got a raw deal, it was my dad. I spoke to him once about the fact that he never saw me play, and I was both stunned and moved to hear him reply to me, "Even though I was not there, before each game I would get down on my knees and pray that God would bring you home safely, free of injury."

I guess I could have done a lot worse. I had plenty of friends that didn't even have dads in their lives. At least I had the memories of my dad teaching me to shave, and of course those wrestling nights. And it used to be even more extreme, as my older sisters have shared many stories about dad's being home even less when they were small. The one story that is legendary in our house is about a time when my dad actually stayed home sick one day from work. My sisters walked into my parents' bedroom and saw my mom sleeping next to a "stranger." They immediately ran upstairs to my grandmother's apartment, yelling hysterically that there was a strange man in bed with mom. My grandmother came running downstairs, broom in hand, ready to take on this intruder. My mom and grandmother had a good laugh, but I can only imagine the sadness that overtook my dad when he realized that his own daughters didn't even know who he was.

I joked in the last chapter that my dad works sixty hours a week at his part-time job, but in reality I am just not sure he knows *how* to slow down. At a time in his life when he should be taking it easy or traveling with my mom, he is always working. He is continuing to miss the truly important things in life. When I go to visit him these days, he is rarely home because, in his "retirement," he works weekends.

But I do see glimpses at times of another side of him. When my niece was born, I watched my dad play with her, trying to make her laugh as he bounced her on his knee. In that moment I realized a couple of things. First, I didn't even recognize this man. He actually seemed to be enjoying himself with the simple pleasure of playing with this small child. If my grandmother still lived upstairs, I think I would have asked her to again grab that broom because there was a "stranger" playing with my niece. But second, it came to me that, given the chance, this is maybe how my dad would have lived his life. Bouncing kids on his knee and getting them to laugh. Instead, he was saddled so young with the responsibility of providing for the family – a huge task that left him little time for anything else. That early responsibility set him on a path – a path full of habits and ways of doing things. Ways that he would find impossible to depart from later in life. It was in that moment that I forgave my dad for missing my childhood and instead thanked him for the role he did play in helping me to become the person I am today. I don't resent the situation we found ourselves in, but accept it for what it is – feeling gratitude for the lessons he has taught me and for all that he has been in my life.

Being There

Although I think that I "get it" – that I have learned the lesson of prioritizing what is important in my life – it is a hard road to the truth, as our society is failing miserably in this area. As I've already noted, people are working longer and longer hours, often even working when they are not at work. So much for the dream of "quality" family time. And for many, the pursuit of success leads into jobs that also require extensive business travel. What good is a giant house or a summer home if you're never there to enjoy it with the people you love? Eventually you will wake up one morning and realize you have missed a big slice of your life – and theirs. Don't be the dad or mom who has only seen your kids' school plays or dance recitals on videotape because you were at work.

During one of my rare business trips, my wife shared a memorable story with me that I often replay in my mind. After I had left the house the morning of my trip, my wife walked into our bedroom to find our then six-year-old daughter in the closet with her nose nuzzled into my shirts. When my wife asked her why on earth she was doing such a funny thing, my daughter said that she missed me already and that the smell of my shirts reminded her of me. Adorable, yes. But I don't want a repeat performance. I want to be there for her, so she can hug *me*, not my wardrobe! The pursuit of luxury could never lead me to go without my daily hugs – or the shouts of "Daddy" when I get home each day.

I hope this chapter seems foreign to most of you. I hope you allow other aspects of your life define who you are – because, if you find yourself being defined by your job, you will unfortunately find room for little else. My dad was defined by what he did for work. He was a great businessman and a great provider. Everything that he has provided for me during my lifetime – both materially and in his sound bits of wisdom that have shaped the way I look at the world – have helped me to become the man I am today.

As for me, though, I wish to be defined by other titles, as well. I want to be known as a great dad. A loving husband. A trusted friend. A faithful Christian. Being a great manager and leader at work does make my top five – but it's number five, not number one. Where my approach to life differs from my dad's is that what I do for my job and career is just one of the things on my "list" – just one of the acts of this play. My job provides my family with a certain lifestyle, for which I am very grateful. But it is not my life. Achieving success at my job will always be important to me, but it will never take center stage.

Final Thoughts

For the managers and would-be managers,
who have read this book for insight…
Look for that mentor who can share bits of wisdom along your journey. It doesn't have to be the most educated, smooth-talking individual on the planet – just someone you trust and whose understanding transcends the mere words he or she speaks.

And always encourage each other to achieve excellence in the office, but also to leave it there at the end of the day. To work at a job we love is an exciting privilege – but it is not life.

For the members of my family,
who have read this because you love me…
I can't promise a lifetime of sunny days. I can't promise that I'll always make the right decisions or have all the answers. But I do promise one thing – that the time I do spend at work will be dedicated to the good of my family. And it will never be more important than the treasured time I share with those closest to me.

And for my dad,
who may not read this at all – because he's lived it...
It's impossible to adequately put into words my thanks for the lessons I have learned from you. Your simple wisdom has lit a fire that inspired these pages, my career, and my life. I will be forever grateful for the chance you have given me to follow in your big footsteps.